ROXANNE HEAD

--Robin T. Chandler

Who is this one-eyed lady,
And what is it she wants?
Her outlook is quite shady;
Suspicious are her haunts.
Hath she perhaps an axe to grind,
Agendas to support?
Is she on watch our sins to find,
Our follies to report?
Does not she add to our dismay
And propagate confusion?
Or does she seek a smoother way,
Devoid of self-delusion?
Nay, friend, feel not a false alarm;
Relax your fears to half.
She does not bring us any harm;
She wants to make us laugh.

Then why does she disquiet me
With subtle words and deep,
That thoughts might come to visit me,
Ideas to my sleep,
Till I hold no illusions more
Of life or love or money?
The naked world, like her, you'll find
Enthralling, sad and funny.

The Satin Thorn

More Poetry of Roxanne Head

ALAN K. BRADBURY

ROXANNE HEAD

ROBIN T. CHANDLER

Library of Congress Control Number: 2019907850

PAPERBACK: 978-1-7337014-8-8
EBOOK: 978-1-7337014-9-5

Ordering Information:

For orders and inquiries, please contact:
1-888-404-1388
www.goldtouchpress.com
book.order@goldtouchpress.com

Printed in the United States of America

Dedicated to Anna Bradbury, with love,
and to the poets of the Harmon's Senior Center
poetry class.

INTRODUCTION
Who is ROXANNE HEAD?

Many years ago I had the honor and privilege of editing Roxy's first book of poetry, *Wisdom and Whimsy*. I'm not particularly proud of my effort, and unsure if I welcome this chance to "redeem" myself. A decade and more has passed; both of us have grown older, and her daughters have moved out. She never did get the job she wanted, as a newspaper columnist. Maybe being older we're wiser now, or maybe just otherwise. She still suffers from acute and chronic conjunctivitis and a bum knee. I've grown arthritic myself, so I can appreciate a little what she goes through getting ready for her day.

Has her poetry improved? She writes more comic verse and less of other kinds, so we'll have to divide the comic verse into chapters now. She still writes songs, usually set to other people's music. And she has asked me to include a few of my own songs, so they will have a short chapter.

As with the original volume, there will be filler at the bottom of pages not taken up by poems, and it will be just as snarky and fun as the first volume—which is still in print at Lulu.com but available only through the author's website, awakenahero.com I hope we can come up with a cover as original and cute as that one had!

For those unacquainted with the first volume, Roxy is fifty-something, on SSI disability and lives alone in Utah, aside from several cats. I don't know why, but writers seem to be required to own at least one enormous housecat. Her Foozy Cat certainly qualifies! Thor, another cat, is a tuxedo Maine Coon, the largest housecat breed in the world. Roxy is covered twice.

Me: Roxy, have you written any new favorite poems?
Roxy: The Lazy Poet is still my best, the one on the back cover of the first book. It won me international prizes in competitions. The Feasters' Daughters won me a $25 prize in a Nevada competition and was published in *Of Unicorns and Space Stations* magazine. It has ceased publication, so we can include it in this volume, along with the poems published by Twin Towers, in *Ramblings of the Wandering Elite*. They're also out of business. The money for FD was five dollars more than Poe got for "The Raven." Of course, $20 was worth a lot more in 1842!

Of my new poems, it all depends on my mood.

Me: Have you grown as a poet?
Roxy: Sideways! The brain doesn't always work as well as it used to. I still want people to go, "Ha! Ha! Huh?" when they read me. I don't think I succeed very often, but try this one:

SONGBIRD

I shall not teach the world to sing
    No songs of joy or glee;
I'd rather that the world come
    And listen now to me!

This one doesn't really fit my style, but I like it anyway:

WISE OLD

My name is Al. I'm getting old.
That doesn't mean my heart is cold;
So if perchance you feel to scowl,
Just call upon the wise old Al.

Roxy: I've noticed I have written some poems that aren't in good
taste. I don't feel proud of this! Toilet humor is always in bad
taste, even when it's funny, and it isn't often funny. This is
an example:

TOILET

Oh, what a smelly mess I make
    When I sit on the toilet.
I must clean up behind myself;
    Nobody will enjoy it.

Me: Roxy, how's your health?
Roxy: Poor. I suspect I may not linger much longer, but take
some consolation from a Jewish proverb: The more you
complain, the longer God makes you live.
Me: I'll live forever, then.
Roxy: And get older and more feeble-minded every year, no doubt.
Well, we can only suffer the afflictions of old age if we're
lucky. I'm not really old, but too decrepit to work at a regular
job anymore. I don't know how much longer I'm going to last!
I want to get this project done and in the hands of a publisher.

Me: How do you want the book structured?
Roxy: Last time we did it according to the type of poem. Let's
do it by subject this time. But, please, start with my songs!
Me: We will.

CHAPTER ONE
SONGS, FILK AND OTHERWISE

We went into some detail about filk songs last time (See *Wisdom and Whimsy*). Basically, it's setting new words to old melodies, and has been around as long as music. This name came from a science fiction convention typo (they meant to put "folk"), and was well enough liked that it stuck. There is even a filk hall of fame!

Roxy has written her share of filk songs, and even filked herself once.

The first one is to be sung to the tune of "If You're Happy and You Know It."

UNTITLED FILK

If you're sickly and you know it, go lay down.
Feeling icky and you show it, go lay down.
    If your nose has come to blows
    And a gickle found your toes
Take a nap and you'll feel better. Go lay down.

If you're healthy and you know it, get to work.
Feeling chipper and you show it, get to work.
    If an eep is on your nose
    Meep it quickly ere it goes.
Get your job done, do it now, just get to work.

In WW there were a few poems about whias and their cousins, whoos and whees. These are hand creatures you can make yourself. They tend to be on the dim side, but manage to work in a lot of fun anyway. The big differences: whoos have tails, whias don't and whees are half as big and much smarter. They curl into rocks to sleep, and some never uncurl. These are called Yocks (again, whiayocks, whooyocks and wheeyocks). Roxy says her poem about whooyocks is her grandkids' favorite (WW p. 60). Some types of whias: gickles (tickle toes), yishes (scratch backs), eeps (sit on other whias' nerdnoses and say, "Eep!"), meeps (squash and eat eeps), ayoomers (eat everything, the name comes from the sound a vacuum cleaner makes), root-a-roots (sailors), shmims (aquatic), reetls (walk lurching side to side like camels), binkers (bounce), and nosers (more about them later).

This is the song wherein she filks her own song "I Told Her No."

DON'T TELL HER NO

If you meet a vampire who's out late in the night,
Who speaks of her love for you, born at first bite,
If she offers embrace, don't refuse at first sight.
    Don't tell her no.
You might not live to see day,
No time for pining away.
    It's not for you.
Don't make a vampire mad;
You won't have time to feel sad
    Unless you're in bondage.

She'll offer you love that will give your heart flight
If you forsake the day and stay up in the night.
Strange powers assure you that she's always right.
    Don't tell her no.

Quick in your mind do the math:
Say yes or suffer her wrath,
     It's not for you.
You'll never stake her, you see;
You don't have celerity.
     Live with your bondage.

Forget about whatever it is you desire.
A neonate's will must be bound to the sire,
So give her your best or you just might expire.
    Don't tell her no.

Another whoo and whee song, to the melody of "Little Bunny Foo Foo."

    Yit'l funny whoo whoo
    Walking through the forest,
    Scooping up the wheeyocks
    And bopping them on the nerdnose.

Along came Whee Yalchemist, and said,

    Yit'l funny whoo whoo,
    Whees don't want to see whoo
    Scooping up the wheeyocks
    And bopping them on the nerdnoses.

Another word about whias and their kin: Each has a bulbous nose like the candy called Nerds. Hence, nerdnoses. Whias are normally timid, but some sit on other whias' nerdnoses and say "Eep!"

The following song was written to be sung to the tune of "The Holy City," a magnificent and majestic work:

MINAS MORGUL

Last night as I read Tolkien,
There came a dream to scare.
I saw old Minas Morgul
With all the nazgul there.
The fields were filled with flowers
That glowed a sickly green,
While all around were orc corps-
Es all scattered on the scene.
While all around were orc corpses
All scattered on the scene.

Minas Morgul! Minas Morgul!
Hark, how the lightning flares!
The ringwraiths on their black stallions,
The nazgul bring the scares.

'Twas once a place of beauty,
The Tower of the Moon.
It's now changed to the ghastly,
With fumes that make one swoon.
The streets are filled with darkness;
The prisons with despair,
While way up in the high pass
You'll find old Shelob's Lair.
While way up in the lofty pass
You'll find old Shelob's lair.

God sends the meat; the devil sends the cooks.

To the tune of "And the Band Played On:"

Grandpa would snuggle his dishwater blonde
    While the alarm blared on.
He would lie 'neath the sheets with the sweetest of sweets
    While the alarm blared on.

What follows is set to John Denver's "Some Days Are Diamond:"

YOCKS

Some yocks are whiayocks; some yocks are whoos.
Sometimes you get yocks that you don't choose.
Sometimes you eat rocks, but that is not news.
Some yocks are whiayocks; some yocks are whoos.

WHOO YOCK THE YIT'L WHOO

(To the tune of Popeye the Sailor Man)

Whoo's Whooyock, the Yit'l Whoo
Whoo's Whooyock, the Yit'l Whoo.
    Whoo's round as a snail
    All but 'cept for Whoo's tail.
Whoo's Whooyock, the Yi-it-l Whoo.

Whias and Whoos have trouble with pronouns, and usually reserve them for personal names. They also have speech defects.

The song that follows is just a song. It wasn't written to a particular melody. For a Dungeons and Dragons® game Roxy elected to play a bard named Tenne ("ten") Mellifluous, a short human (5'3"), and wrote this song about him:

LITTLE BIG

We need a song to ease our care
    And help the night along,
To make our bitter ale taste sweet
    We need a cheerful song:
And that's where little Tenne comes up big
    That's where he comes up big.

When troubles abound and you've no idea
    When next your pint will refill,
Just ask for help from nearby friends
    And see which ones are real.
And that's when little Tenne comes up big;
    That's when he comes up big.

When loneliness comes over you
    And you need the hand of love,
A pat on the back, an encouraging word,
    The comfort of a hug,
That's when little Tenne comes up big;
    That's when he comes up big.

KITCHEN SIGNS:
A messy kitchen is a happy kitchen, and this one is delirious!
No husband has ever been shot while doing the dishes.
If we are what we eat, I'm easy, fast and cheap.
A balanced diet is a cookie in each hand.
Thou shalt not weigh more than thy refrigerator.
A clean house is a sign of a misspent life.
Complaints about the cooking can be hazardous to your health.
My next house will have no kitchen – just vending machines.

When Roxy gets into the mood, she writes a lot of the same kind
of poems, such as filk songs in 2010. This is the most recent one:

ON MARS

(to Tchaikovsky's First Piano Concerto)

While on the planet of Mars
Beneath an orange sky with stars,
    My spacesuit sprang a leak
    And when I took a peek
A green-skinned Martian was there
Who restored me my air.

He was making a show
And asked before I could go
    What kind of music we of Earth liked best.
    I told him, "Filk,"
And sang him this song.

You know what I did before I got married? Anything I wanted!
    --Henny Youngman
I am not paid enough to be nice to you.

MOM'S GONNA MURDER ME

I'm going to the bridge above the river.
I'm going where the water's blue and brown.
I'm going where the sunlight sparkles silver,
I'm going to trip and fall clean off and drown.

I'm going to the fancy new cathedral,
The one that took a hundred years to build.
I'll climb the stairs and look out from the belfry,
And slip and on the cobblestones be killed.

I've got my bow and I am going hunting,
To get some meat so I can fix my sup.
I'll find the boar, the bear, the lynx and lion;
Together they are going to eat me up.

I'm going to clobber Jack, the neighbor bully,
And pound and mash and kick him into dreck;
But if I take too long to win the battle
He'll trip me on the curb and break my neck.

The guards are on their way to come arrest me,
Because they say I stolen goods have portered;
Although I claim I never did that,
The king is going to have me drawn and quartered.

So many times by bullies I've been slaughtered,
Or else by accident I have been slain,
That I'm afraid to go home to my momma
For fear she's going to murder me again.

HINGES FILK   (TO THE TUNE OF "HINGES")

Whoo's all made of tail because everything yiggles
From the tip of Whoo's rump to the pygmi that giggles.
When Whoo wants to yiggle tail Whoo can just choose
Faster and shmeeter than all nother Whoos.

Whia is all made of nerdnose because everything freeks
From the tips of Whias' eyeballs to the end of Whias' beaks
Nothing stays hidden from Nosers, you see—
Whias found San Diego out west by the sea.

Pygmi: a whia as tiny as the period at the end of a sentence; they
   tend to swarm. Like tribbles from StarTrek, they are born
   pregnant.

The poem that follows is a filk song, to be sung to Johnny
Horton's "Sink the Bismarck."

THE BALLAD OF GRISLY DAN

This is the tale of Grisly Dan, a robber in the wood,
Who preyed upon rich travelers and did them nothing good.
He lived a merry life until some soldiers him espied,
And then upon a gallows-tree ignominiously died.

When he was but a callow youth his first life he did take,
And then the company of men he must with haste forsake;
So sought he refuge in the trees where hidden glens abound
And there he hoped to live his life and never more be found.

For three long years he laid him low and lived just off the land,
With trusty bow he shot the deer, caught partridges by hand,
But then he felt an awful thirst and knew he must have wine:
So hid he by the highway side and robbed a merchant fine.

So skilled at robbery and death he soon enough became
That folks went miles out of their way to add not to his fame.
Then came a soldier him to catch and fought with sword and spear,
But Grisly Dan cut him in half and lopped the soldier's ear.

Thrice more in winter Dan killed men who traveled all alone,
Till none would go without a troop of guards to guard their own.
A hated thief and murderer, by all most feared and sought,
All clad in skins, and with his bow he swore he'd not be caught.

At last one day in sunny spring a merchant band came by,
All fat old men with loaded wains and coin-bags for the eye.
The grisly robber leaped to steal, but much to his surprise
They were a band of soldiers bold, each wearing a disguise.

They took the grisly killer to the judge within the town;
And all the people came to see the man who'd made them frown.
They gnashed their teeth and cursed and heaped on Grisly Dan
their shame,
But everyone gave out a cheer when gallows made its claim.

So let this be a lesson to all callow youths with fire:
Do not go killing folks for fun or for your profit's hire.
Don't do bad things to make you hide midst pine or fir or spruce—
For soldiers certainly will come and make for you a noose.

Open yourself to criticism. A fine polish requires abrasive.
        --Marie vos Savant

Roxy played another bard, Gunnar, and wrote several songs as him. Grisly Dan may or may not be one of them; it's in the same part of her diaries. The following definitely are Gunnar songs:

THE MINSTREL

"What do you offer, you young, skinny fool?
    What can you offer to me ere you go?"
"I offer you beauty and food for your soul,
    A respite of cheer in your lifetime of woe."

AUBURN

She had the reddest, darkest hair
    And wonderful green eyes;
So when I saw her sitting there
    I marshalled my best lies,
And came and introduced myself.
    She smiled and waved me on.
She said to "go pack off thyself,
    Leave me, and just be gone."

I said, "Why do you say such things?
    You don't know what I want!
I've not said yet to you what brings
    Me to your quiet haunt."
"You bards are all alike," she quoth,
    "With one thought on your mind:
To talk sweet till you've won my troth,
    Bed me and leave behind

"Perhaps a bairn for me to raise
    While you no help impart,
But e'en if not, at least there stays
    My achy, broken heart.
You have your fun and move along
    With timbrel, harp and waltz.
Of love that's true you build your song,
    But your love's always false."

A sadder but no wiser man,
    I go upon my way.
I know she's right; 'spite and plan
    A bard can never stay.
A life of loss and loneliness

    Is all we can afford,
For we must seek new audience
    Whenever ours gets bored.

    I've tried to set that song to Fleetwood Mac's "Rhiannon," but it doesn't quite fit. The next song must also have its own melody:

RIDING HORSES

When life begins to be a grind
And nowhere is there peace of mind,
The way to solace is, I find,
        Riding horses.

[interlude at a walking gait]

When enemies accumulate
And swords grow thick around the gate,
I must flee swiftly, and not wait,
        Riding horses.

[interlude at a trot]

The way to win a maiden's heart
And bind it so you'll never part,
Is woo her, please her, let her start
        Riding horses.

[interlude at a gallop]

The more things change, the more they remain—insane.

ACCORDING TO OLD GRANDPA

When I was just a little tyke I used to go and sit
Myself down by the rocking chair where Grandpa sat a bit,
And told the weirdest stories until all the crows would caw
      According to old Grandpa.

He whittled me a whistle with the strangest little knife
That any could imagine in a fascinating life.
He got it from space aliens, the weirdest ever saw—
      According to old Grandpa.

Once he met a grizzly bear while tramping in the hills
Who reached a paw, and saved him when o'er a cliff he spills.
He thanked the bear in person then, and shook him by the claw—
      According to old Grandpa.

Once a cat went hunting whias within his own front yard,
And purty nearly captured one, although that's mighty hard.
But Grandpa chased the lynx away, which made the whia go "Taa!"
      According to old Grandpa.

Grandpa fought a mountain once, and pounded it to sand.
The wind then blew it all away into another land.
Mashing up them boulders sure did make his knuckles raw—
      According to old Grandpa.

The number that follows is a traditional folksong, popular at summer camps. Numerous versions exist. Roxy does not claim this song, like Kelly Brady claimed "500 Miles." Lesley Nelson Burns and Mary Tyson both claim its authorship, but their chaotic messes are undated. Both used the lines about horses with feet on the ground and peeping through the knothole, and Tyson's version has the lines about the snake's necktie. It's in the public domain. But Roxy did rework the lyrics so they'd make a little more sense to her.

A BOY'S BEST FRIEND   --PUBLIC DOMAIN

While peeping through the knothole
In Grandpa's wooden leg
    I thought I saw my sister kiss a turtle (A turtle!?)
Go get the Listerine! Sister has a beau,
    And a boy's best friend is his mother.

While looking out the window,
The second-story window,
    I slipped and bruised my eyebrow on the pavement.
Go get the axe, there's a hair on baby's chin!
    And a boy's best friend is his mother.

The horses run around
With their feet upon he ground.
    Why did they build the shore so near the ocean?
Go get the tweezers! There's a flea in baby's ear,
    And a boy's best friend is his mother.

The stars were shining brightly
Although it isn't nighty.
    Who will wind the clocks while I am gone?
Go get the spray; there's a fly on baby's chest,
    And a boy's best friend is his mother.

While walking in the moonlight,
The bright and sunny moonlight,
    She kissed me on the eye with a tomato.
A snake's belt will slip because he has no hips,
    And Grandma's false teeth will soon fit Jenny.

Noted pyromaniac Arson Wells
A pregnant dog is full of puppies. That's the best!
I never travel without my diary. One should always have something sensational to read.
    --Oscar Wilde
The girl who stayed too long under the sunlamp is now the toast of the town.
What happens in Vegas stays on Facebook
I'm like anybody else – only with fewer active ingredients
The boarding house blew up. Roomers were flying everywhere.
She's the kind who takes dirty old men to the cleaners.
Tequila = the gulp of Mexico
I look like a million dollars – all wrinkly and green
She got her looks from her father—mostly looks of disappointment.
If you have a lot of tension, do what it says on the aspirin bottle: "Take two tablets" and "Keep away from children."
If flying is so safe, why is the airport called a terminal?
When I was young I went "skinny-dipping." Now I "chunky-dunk."
Every time I walk into a singles bar I hear Mom's words: "Don't pick that up! You don't know where it's been!"
Clean up after yourself – Mom's off duty.

CHAPTER TWO
CAT CALLS

Like me, Roxy is a cat fancier and has owned several cats over the years. Three of her current felines were dropped off by her daughters: Miss Boots, Thor and Tig. She's had Foozy Cat several years longer, but it wouldn't surprise me if she came from a daughter as well. Wanting to write a second book of poetry, she turned to her mousers for inspiration.

Cats are the only "domesticated" animal that adopted humans instead of the other way around. As every cat owner knows, no one owns a cat. Another tidbit of cat wisdom: Cats taught curiosity to men, but retained sense for themselves. These are in no particular order:

FOOZY CAT

I tot I taw a puddy tat, and she was decked with fooze.
At contests being finicky, she can never lose.
When it's *Gata*-spoiling time, why, I'm the one she'll choose
Except when hiding from the kids or curled up a-snooze.

MESSY BOOTS REDUX

I tot I taw a puddy tat who had four messy boots.
She came with whiskers on her nose and fur upon her glutes.
Whenever cats begin to fight, she's always in cahoots.
I think I'll toss her in the wash and down the laundry chutes.

CAT FLEAS

I tot I taw a puddy tat. Its fleas were white as snow,
And everywhere the puddy went, the fleas were sure to go.
I gave the puddy tat a bath; the fleas were hopping mad—
And now I itch all over me and hate the fleas so bad!

PUDDY TAT

I tot I taw a puddy tat who's craving to get spoiled,
Yet human hands must not touch her, and so her want is foiled.
She will not catch a bird or mouse, but miaows to be fed.
Leave the door ajar and she'll your rug and sofa shred.

THOR   (WRITTEN BEFORE HE MOVED IN)

I tot I taw a puddy tat, and he was decked with hair.
With his huge head and big, fat paws he might have been a bear,
Save for his long and bushy tail, with which
He can do nothing but lay it out and twitch.

Thor is a Maine Coon, the largest housecat breed, and has paws
that might make a bear jealous. But he frequently gets his tail
stepped on. He loves to lay in high traffic areas where he can
wrangle some spoiling, as we'll see soon.

LET THE CATS OUT

There are no *gatos* in the house.
Your husband let them out, dear spouse.
If only we could find a way
To keep them out, 'twould be okay.

The word "okay" meaning "yes" has an interesting history and numerous theories
as to how it came to be part of our lexicon. Some say many captured German papers
after World War One had OK stamped on them for the German *Oberkommandant*.
Another theory dates it to Martin Van Buren's election, which was supported by an
OK Club. Actually, it started as a Choctaw word, "okeh," meaning "amen" or "so
be it."

SPOILED THOR

Our black puddy tat, name of Thor,
Got petted while stretched on the floor.
    And as he got stroked,
     His purring invoked
A plea to get spoiled some more.

MISS BOOTS (ORIGINAL)

I tot I taw a puddy tat who had four messy boots.
She came with whiskers on her nose and fur upon her glutes.
Averse to spoiling, still she'll rest on someone's nice, warm knee.
She's old and cranky, loves to fight, and acts obnoxiously.

In this town there's nothing doing every minute of the day!
Scouts are gathering aluminum and other items for recycling. Proceeds will be used
to cripple children.

STAND-OFFISH CAT

My cat, who customarily regards me with disdain,
And should I want to spoil her, she loudly will complain;
But when I want MY "litter box" and sit upon the "throne"
She's here demanding spoiling and won't leave me alone.

TIG'S POEM

I tot I taw a puddy tat, Obnoxious Orange by name.
A door that's closed? He's on the wrong side; at least that is his claim.
He has a smooth and silky coat, which brings that cat no fame
'Cause he's averse to being spoiled—what a shame!

MESSY BOOTS

Messy Boots, Messy Boots, why are your boots a mess?
I don't know; I don't know; stepped in crud I guess.
Messy Boots, Messy Boots, give your boots a shine.
No no no, no no no; messy boots are fine.

FOR/ABOUT THOR:

I tot I taw a puddy tat who had the fattest paws,
And what can be the use of them is more than Arkan saws,
He wants his mistress, Tiffany, so he can get quite spoiled,
But she is out of town this week, and so his want is foiled.

Roxy apologized for reusing a rhyme.

FOR/ABOUT TIG:

I tot I taw a puddy tat who's lying on the couch.
He has the teeth and curving claws that make my skin go, "Ouch!"
He has a soft and smooth orange pelt that I would love to pet,
But he's obnoxious and aloof and hasn't let me yet.

SNEEZY YOCK   (THIS IS MISS BOOTS)

I tot I taw a puddy tat who was a sneezy yock.
Whenever she began to sneeze, she'd sneeze around the clock.
She would not go outside to play, lest other kitties mock;
But if they do, why, knowing her, their blocks she off will knock.

ELRIC'S POEM

A kitten came to our abode, and Elric was his name.
He didn't have just foozy pelt, but with a mane he came.
While other cats are purr-faced, have stripes or patch or mange,
Our Elric had a special gift—the cat could shed at range!

I ate five nickels today to feel the change in myself.
Is Congress the only place you can phone and never get a busy signal?
When I was born, the stork made a crash landing.
It was a formal wedding – Pa even painted the shotgun white.
Mixed emotions: seeing your mother-in-law drive off a cliff in your new Cadillac…
I was cleaning the chimney, slipped and came down with the flue.

CHAPTER THREE
HAIKU

The haiku is a poetic form of Japan which has caught on in America. While some churn them out by the ream, Roxy doesn't use the form often. In the hands of a master, like Japanese poet Izzu or cartoon character Zuko, they can be very moving and even funny. Roxy tends to keep her haiku serious and at least tries to follow the forms.

ROMANCE

You shine so brightly
I long to be beside you:
Basking glow of love.

BLUE

The sun and the sky:
A world of endless blue waits,
Beckoning to me.

LESS THAN SIGNIFICANT

I am a pebble.
No one will notice if I
Disappear from view.

Praise the Lord and pass the ammunition.   --Rev. Howell Porgy
There are no traffic jams on the road to repentance.
          --Neil A. Maxwell

REPENTANCE

Missionaries craft
A mighty change of heart in
Those who hear their words.

INN-FATUATION

Eating my midday,
Watching the lady with the
Newspaper stroll past.

FLUTTERBY

Fancy flits and flut-
Ters like a butterfly on
The wing. My thoughts, too.

TUBE STEAK II

I get a hot dog
Topped with relish and mustard.
I call it tube steak.

SQUASHAGE

The sausage sizzles
On the grill while I'm waiting:
My favorite song!

Never tell people how to do things. Tell them what to do, and their ingenuity will surprise you.   --Gen. George S. Patton

Everything you want is just outside your comfort zone.
         --Robert Allen
Are we looking down in fear or up in faith?
Happiness is a warm bubble bath.
Nowadays the man who has everything needs help with making the payments.
My car left without me.
Home is where you go when all the other joints are closed.
"When did you learn to weave?" "When I followed Rudyard Tippling home one night."
"How could you break a tooth on a cheese sandwich?" "You left the mousetrap in it."
Few people understand Einstein, but nobody understands me.
The pool is open every day but Monday. That's when we wash the dishes.

CHAPTER FOUR
PHILOSOPHICAL POEMS

I expect there to be quite a few of these, poems that make one go "huh?" Well-done, they can be extremely charming and delightful, but as usual the quality may be inconsistent.

A WRITER OF FANTASY

A writer of fantasy must live apart,
For worlds without number dwell in his heart;
And there for a part of each day he must dwell
Conceiving adventures like FK and Rell;
But then to Tellurian he must return
To write what his musings have brought him to learn.
    *FK = Faerie King, a fantasy novel

A CHILD'S GRACE

Please bless those who keep me fed,
Medium well, not too red.

[That might not be Roxy's]

SCHOOL

Wakey wakey rise and drool;
It is time to go to school.
Wakey wakey rise and groan,
No more snoozing all alone.

LONESOME HUSBAND'S LAMENT

My sweetheart will not come to bed
And snuggle with her man. Instead
She crochets blankets by TV
And seldom ever thinks of me.

SNOOZY ROCK

The favorite thing that this Whia views
Is back of eyelids while a-'nooze.

POET'S LAMENT

Here I am at the end of the line.
My feet are up; I'm feeling fine.
Just one thing makes me feel worse:
This wretched urge to cobble verse.

LITTLE BOY YELLOW

Little boy yellow, go flee the yard.
A bully is coming who's strong and hard.
Where is the boy who won't exercise?
Playing a video game while in disguise.

It's the fire alarm – somebody just got fired.
If sins did not dim the brain, nobody would ever get married, drunk or fat.
   --Orson Scott Card
When the tin man was run over by a steam roller, he said, "Curses! Foiled again!"
Remember in prayer those who are sick of our church and community…
On the line that asks what you made last year, put "trouble"
What's the difference between a Harley and a Hoover? The location of the dirt bag.

STRIPLING WARRIOR

A youth who could fight like a dragon, I'm told,
Was dubbed as a knight though but thirteen years old.
Castle, lands, stables he won, and much more—
What will this kid do for an encore?

TEN POEM QUEST

I want to write ten pomes today.
The form doesn't matter;
Rhymed or unrhymed,
Structured or free,
Long or short,
As long as they're on different topics.
Maybe one of them will be good,
Sporting memorable phrases and eliciting memorable emotions.
Maybe one of them will live.

LIGHT

The light does more than let us see;
    It helps us understand,
And when it comes on in our brain,
    Why, doesn't that feel grand?

POKER

The deck is like a calendar, a card for every week.
Four suits are like four seasons. Jokers we all seek.
The odds are stacked against us, in favor of the house,
And yet we draw to inside straights like any foolish louse.

PENCIL

What will come forth from this gray stick—
Some words profound, or scribbly ick?
Foul words or inspiration's voice?
It's not the pencil makes the choice.

SQUIRRELY

I need some advice, and hope you won't mind,
    But can tell me how this story ends:
If I go to St. Louis and leave it behind,
    Will my squirrel and I still be friends?

The following poem was inspired by a quote attributed to
Robin Hood:

INSPIRATION

The man who reaches for a star,
Although he may not get that far,
Still reaches higher than the sods
Who stoop for trash among the clods.

WISDOM

Prepare yourself ahead of time
    And use some wise discretion.
You never get a second chance
    To make a first impression.

HOME

When thinking on some words I said,
Home is where I hang my head.

PICKY AND TIRED

I'm picky and I'm tired.
Make my eggs over hard.

MY SWEETHEART'S CARE

How spoiled are my feet and knee—
My sweetheart takes good care of me.

SIMPLE WISH

I wish I were gorgeous, athletic and young,
Also, richer than kings and much better hung;
With brains like Nic Tesla and wisdom like God—
Then life's tedious paths would be easily trod.

There is now a section of holiday poems:

THE FOUR MAIN CELTIC HOLIDAYS

Imbolc - when the lambs are born
Beltane – by when sheep are shorn
Lammas – when the pasture's high
Samhain   when the seasons die

ALL FOOLS' DAY

What can I say
Of April Fools' Day—
Our favorite day of the year—
We raise it no fuss
'Cause it's about us,
So let's celebrate with good cheer.

When life becomes more than you can stand—kneel.
My pussycat ate a ball of yarn – and had mittens!
Communicate with fish by dropping them a line.

GROUNDHOG DAY

On Imbolc, when the ground hog
    His shadow would espy,
To see if spring will soon arrive
    Or if more snow will fly;
In olden days it was the time
    When little lambs were born,
So they can drink their mother's milk
    While ewe and ram eat corn.
But now this ancient holiday
    Has gone degenerate,
So only Punxatawny Phil
    Can forecast winter's fate.

10TH OF MAY

When it becomes the tenth of May
We'll celebrate a holiday,
And it will be one we like—
For we can drive a golden spike.

Other poets can write about Mother's Day and Christmas,
Thanksgiving and Independence Day. Roxy writes about more
obscure holidays which can be more fun.

I'm in love with 14 soldiers, but it's only platoonic.
The dilemmas of childhood are the dilemmas of all life: Belonging and betrayal, the
power of the group and the courage it takes to be an individual.   --J. K. Rowling
Zero tasking = doing nothing
Steel is strong because it has known the hammer and high heat.
The moth ate the rug to see the floor show.

THE ONLY THING YOU CAN DO WITH A PAIR OF GLOVES ON IS WET YOUR PANTS
(--farm proverb)

My father's words in my mind churn;
Without the gloves I get rope burn,
Splinters, road rash, scrape-ups, too—
I'll put mine on now. Wouldn't you?

RHYMES WITH LINOLEUM

Partaking of petroleum
Lands you in a mausoleum.

IMPERFECT PAST

I'm the source of the sorrows
That trouble your tomorrows.

WILD FLORA

I cultivate wild flowers
    From blossoms to their seeds.
They fill my yard and garden—
    But please don't call them weeds!

SNACK ON COMPANY TIME

A can of ravioli in meaty 'mater sauce
Will satisfy my hunger and irritate my boss.

THE FROG

A frog unto his sweetheart spoke:
"We'll be together till we croak."
But you and I beat this with glee
For we shall love eternally.

FINE ART

I painted a picture to hang in my home.
I tried to do well; it came out monochrome.

MORNING CALL

Wakey, wakey, rise and groan!
No more snoozing all alone.
Morning sun has come at last,
So it's time to break your fast.

Roxy's youngest daughter had some words with prefixes like bi-, tri-, semi- and mid-, and was assigned for school to write a riddle about one of them. Roxy wrote her three examples:

I   If there's no parachute on thee,
      This is a dreadful place to be.   (mid-air)
II   If we win, there's one more game to play.
      If we lose, we're going home today.   (semifinals)
III   Ben Franklin first invented me
      So his old eyes could clearly see.   (bifocals)

BLADDER CONTROL

I'm always quite thirsty so I piddle a lot.
They say diabetes is what I have got.
I pour in at the top and it flows out the bottom.
For thirst and for drips, why, surely I got 'em!

Roxy calls herself a 4-eyed, no-horned, writing purple peeps ayoomer.
Everything happens for a reason, and sometimes the reason is that you're a
numbskull.   --Brian Crane

The next three poems were written under a fictitious identity.
Roxy wrote a story about a farm boy, then wrote these poems
as if the farm boy, Connor, had written them.

PLOW HORSE

The horse that pulls the plow,
    A strong and placid beast,
He cannot race no how,
    And doesn't mind the least.
We honor him a lot
    For all his daily toil.
Without him we could not
    Begin to till the soil.

THE SEED

Within the ground awaits the seed
For spring to sprout into a weed.
Why cannot all our crops and flowers
Grow with such amazing powers?

THE FARMER

The farmer rises ere the sun
    With lots of energy, inspired
To get his morning chores all done.
    What gets he for all this? Just tired.

TUBBY OR NOT

Fatty fatty two by four—
Wait, that's a rather skinny board!
Fatty fatty sixty-four
Around the waist—now that's a hoard!

OUT WEST

When the bloom is on the sage
Then my nose gets in a rage.
The problem is, you see,
I have an allergy.

THESE KIDS AINT GOT NO BEHAVIOR

Duckity pluckity cluck
The kids have run amok.
    Screw their thumbs
    And spank their bums
Until they cry in shock.

LITTLE VANDALS

Tom was on the street.
Some old friends he did meet.
    They ran about
    To scream and shout
And on the fence to beat.

STAND UP

Petey was mad at Irene.
At the square dance last Friday night
She stood her ex-boyfriend up
And he didn't think that was right.
"How could you?" he yelled, and she said,
"Pete, you were drunk as a clown!
The reason I stood you up
Was because you kept falling down."

I believe in life after death, except in Pennsylvania.
"You can't carry a 350# woman!" "I took two trips."

REVISITED NURSERY RHYME

Puddy tat, mouser, you refried old bean,
Have you been to London to visit the queen?
Puddy tat, mouser, at what do you stare?
The royal canary perched high on the chair.

WILD ODDITY

While riding in the brush I saw
    A sight that made me blink,
For, rustling in a thicket raw
    I caught a glimpse of pink.

Now I know critters black and gray,
    And critters white and brown,
But pink ones? There just ain't no way!
    The vision made me frown.

I drew my gun and snuck up close
    To peer through green, perhaps,
And in the shrubbery old Mose
    Was pulling up his chaps.

FLY SWATTER

While coming home from the slaughter
I purchased a sturdy fly swatter,
The kind that can take a shellacking
    And keep on whacking.

When nothing's going right, go left.
No one is protected by ignorance.   --Morgan Llewellen
When the leaves drop in autumn, who puts them back on again come spring? The releaf society.

CHAPTER FIVE
MISCELLANEOUS POEMS

Many of these are of poorer quality, and most hardly fit into categories like we've been trying to do all along. But there are gems among the dross, as usual.

TRAVIS AS A SMALL BOY

Travis has a mouth and nose,
Belly button and some toes.
What he does with all this stuff
We can figure right enough:
When he isn't sleeping stiff
He is getting in mischief.

KFC

Oh what a greasy mess I make
When of friend chicken I partake.

CRABBY WHOO SONG

Whoo's name is Crabby Apple Whoo.
    Whoo's rotten to the core.
Give Whoo the schmeetest apple now
    Or Whoo will sing some more.

ENTERTAINER TO THE CROWN

I entertained a handsome prince
By telling jokes that made him wince.
He threw me in the dungeon cell,
Where I'm still rotting. Fare-thee-well!

THE PELICAN IN ITS PIETY

The pelican sits with its beak at its breast.
Drops of blood dribble into the nest.
For this is the sea bird for piety sung—
But that isn't how she feeds her young.

TOAD'S ADVENTURE

My Volkswagen Beetle, whose name was called Toad,
Did follow a Jeep putting up an old road.
The Jeep had to bull its way up through a stream
To get to the highway within my night dream.

A GAME OF CHESS

How can you pull a subtle bluff
    Or fool with moves toward
Some hidden goal worth enough
    With all the pieces on the board?

IF YOU SIT IN A DRAFT OR GET CHILLED

The ague
Will plague you.

GALOSH

One of a pair
Of wet weather wear.

COURTSHIP

A maiden sure will be impressed
By square male jaw and massive chest.
Washboard abs and narrow waist
Are sure to get a fellow chased.
The deepest pockets in the land
At luring maidens sure work grand.
But if you'd cling to wedded bliss
You'll need to do lots more than this.

BIRFUNDAY FILK

We're glad its whoo's birfday, O whooyock.
Happy birfday! Happy birfday to whoo!
We'll sing whoo a song for whoo's birfday:
Sappy birfday! Sappy birfday to whoo!

WHOOYOCK IN GLUE

There once was a whooyock named Whooyock;
Got stuck in some glue and was Gooyock.
    How did it break loose?
    It yiggled caboose,
And got kicked by a boot like a shoeyock.

ONE A.M. BLADDER CALL

Tinkle, tinkle little wee.
How I wonder where you be?
Hiding in my rolls of fat,
Surely there is where you're at.
Hiding, lest I try to aim
Your stream where it will cause no shame
Nor heap embarrassment on me—
Tinkle, tinkle little wee.

SWEET BAD CHESS

My king-side onslaught
With peril was fraught
But it all came to naught
When defense was got.
    Now I'm shot.

["Sweet bad cess to you" is a famous Irish curse.]

FIRELIGHT

In the firelight I see
Memories burning with my home;
For it's my house that's aflame.
From now on I'll have to roam.

DUTY CALLS

When you do as I command
Every task that comes to hand,
Only then will your deeds stand
For accomplishments so grand.

{The previous poem and the following were written for the poetry class Roxy teaches.}

DUTY II

When chores come up by the thousand,
And I'm feeling drained by demand,
I go and relax in the bandstand
And rest till I'm feeling quite bland.

Bad street names: Drinkand Drive, Vicious Circle, Psycho Path, No Friggin Way, Wormwood Drive

ULTIMATE SNAX

Some turkey sliced perky,
    With imitation mayo,
A smackerel of mackerel
    And milk and cookie rodeo,
        Some sliced wheat bread with leaven,
        And I will be in heaven.

AGED POET

Old as the hills and twice as dusty—
No wonder all my poems are rusty!

NEW FLY SWATTER
(SING TO "THIS OLD HOUSE")

Aint goona chase those flies no longer;
Aint gonna chase those flies no more.
I will swat them on the table;
I will swat them on the floor.
I will swat them on the ceiling

And upon the window pane.
I'll put screens up on the doorways
So they won't bug me again.

We want to see if you're human or a space alien. Is there lead in your pants, gold in your teeth and silver in your hair?
Trelawny and I have been dead these past two years, but we don't choose to make it known.   --Lord Chesterfield
Diogenes struck the father when the son swore. –Robert Burton
Are these numbers upper case or lower case?
When British politician Michael Foot was put in charge of a nuclear disarmament committee, the Times wrote: Foot Heads Arms Body
For most of history, anonymous was a woman. –Virginia Woolf
My name is Microsoft. Can I crash at your house tonight?
I underslept last night.   --Dik Browne

FOR TIFFANY

Enthusiasm makes me spasm.
   Vigor wears me out.
Optimism is a prism,
   All but rose blocked out.
A dose of joy does me annoy.
   Cheer makes me see red.
I'll be a grouch here on my couch
   Or take myself to bed.

A YEAR OF RANCID RHYMES

January: schmanuary
February: Ain't it scary?
A long March makes you parch.
In April, rain it will.
In the merry month of May all the folks come out to play.
Come June, we'll swoon.

July: we fry
In the hot August, bake ourselves we must.
September: dismember
My, how fleetly I disrobe her in the bleak October.
Sere November, what a mess! Eleventh twelfth of a weariness.
In December, Christ's birth we cheer.

HOW TO FIX AN AIRPLANE

Put some mucilage
On the fuselage.

FEELINGS

I feel, I feel, I feel like the evening sun.
I feel, I feel, I feel like my work is done.
I feel, I feel, I feel like my race is run.
I feel, I feel, I feel like I weigh a ton.

THE NURSE

We see them at their best when we are feeling worse,
And that's why we oft take a turn for the nurse.

CYNTHIA

O Cynthia, won't you relent
And give me encouragement?
You know I am heels over head,
But you're dating Johnny instead.

BEES-BOL

I love a game of baseball
    And rooting for my team.
Although they're cellar dwellers,
    A fan can always dream.

CELLAR RELICS

In the cellar one can find
    Some old, neglected stuff,
Like spiders, dirt and tater sacks
    And old junk worn and rough.
Among the things we've left behind
    Like shoes bedecked with stuff,
You'll find my favorite baseball team
    To irritate enough.

IRATE PIRATES

"Avast, ye lubbers!" Captain cried,
And on his cutlass then we died.
Our loot we yielded to his crew;
As dead men, what else could we do?
They scuttled us to make us sink,
A watery grave down in the drink.
To ocean's depths we now descend,
And there as squid food we will end.

TIFFANY'S CHORE

T's mopping the floor under Whoo,
And making it sparkle, it's true.
She's hoping that those black spots will all be lifted, too—
Moping the floor under Whoo.

WELCOME TO MISSOURI

Are you a tourist? Come to me!
Missouri loves your company.

TAUNT

I see root beer! I see Squirt®!
I see grandpa's undershirt!

PETROGLYPHS   [ALL CAN BE FOUND IN UTAH]

A six-horned beast first seen
In Utah rock-art scene,
In fossils later found
In rocks beneath the ground;
Uintathere it's called;
Pre-ice-age time it stalled.

These petroglyphs, they say,
For centuries on display,
Except that center one, of course,
The one that shows the horse.
There were no horses here, they say,
In AD 500—no way!

And what of this peculiar art
Of men with—what's this part?
Helmets like a spaceman wears?
Antennae sprouting up in pairs?
Don't say the Injuns wandered stars,
For they were ancestors of ours.

[All are in Nine Mile Canyon, Carbon County, Utah, or in the
Parowan Gap in southern Utah.]

ROACHES I

A roach on the wall
Will let itself fall
Should it feel in danger
From some human stranger.

ROACHES II

A cockroach climbing on a wall
Will trust its wings, let go and fall
If it feels in mortal danger
From some pesky human stranger.

ALL BEETLES HAVE WINGS

A bed bug is not loathe to fly,
Unlike the roach, which hates to try.

BANE SIDHE

Don't listen to the banshee's wail
Or you might be the next in hell.

FAT IS WHERE IT'S AT

It's more than a stomach; this thing is my friend.
It gives aid and blessing that never will end.
It opens a path for me through the crowd,
And sometimes it gurgles and rumbles out loud.
My tummy's great size means it cannot be beat.
Come, gut, and I'll get you a tidbit to eat.

INJURY REPORT

Whene'er you suffer sprains and strains,
You will find your aches and pains
Are at their most severe and worst
Upon the third day, not the first.

MEDICAL PROGNOSIS

The doctor said pharynx
But really meant larynx,
Discoursing on the cancer in my throat.
I wish he'd decided
Which held growths inside it,
Lest he take out the wrong one, and gloat.

SQUATTING IN YOUR SPURS

The cowboy's eyes popped, and he leaped
    While squatting in his spurs.
She heard him yelp and when she peeped,
    By golly, so did hers!

PIERRE AND HIS BIG BROTHER

"Pierre, our father wants to know
    Why you now feel so bad."
"Tell him the way he's treating me
    Is driving me quite mad.

"Whenever I would have some fun
    He always tells me no.
When I want most to meet someone,
    He never lets me go."

"Pierre, you're quite the little boy.
    Much mischief you do make.
You do not own a single toy
    You haven't tried to break.

"You do not treat our things with care
    Or to most folks be kind.
Until you can behave yourself,
    Our father you must mind."

IRISH PROVERBS:
May you live as long as you want, and never want as long as you live.
A change of work is as good as a rest.
The work praises the man.
Making the beginning is one-third of the work.

HUSBANDS

Breathes there a man with soul so boiled
That he wouldn't like to be quite spoiled?
Who wouldn't scratch his itchy back,
Who of massages feels no lack?
Who doesn't want his food prepared
By first rate chef who really cares?
Who wouldn't want this in his life?
Then that's the man who needs no wife.

DIRE REAR   (TUNE: I'VE GOT SPURS)

I've got bowels that gurgle, gurgle, gurgle,
As I race desperately to the "throne."
And they say, "We don't think he will make it;"
And that song ain't so very far from wrong.

3AM ROACH HUNT

Rub a dub dub, twelve roaches in the tub,
And who do you think they be?
The hatchling, the breeder are filthy invaders.
Help squash all the bugs that we see!

WHY YOU CAN'T STAY MAD AT HIM

This guy's
Disguise
Won't let
You get
The pique
You seek.

You will never plough a field if you only turn it over in your mind.
Idleness is a fool's desire.
A quiet tongue shows a wise head.

INCIDENT AT MURPH'S

I was hanging out with stranger guys,
All drinking beer and chomping fries,
When visions from above me came—
Not heaven's light, but jet aflame.
I cried, "Let's all get out of here!
Death is too much to pay for beer!"
I was the first and last to go.
"Who heeds me not ends up below!"
The jet on fire crashed not the bar
To leave a smashed and smoking scar.
The men all got into a fight
To see which one would have the right
To polish off my brewski brown.
Now all their widows wear a frown.

HOW DO THOSE CANDY "COUGH DROPS" WORK?

We suspect
Placebo effect.

MY BEARD

Shaving is annoying; I'll let my beard grow out
Until it reaches chest or waist or somewhere thereabout.
It hides my multitude of chins; it is distinguished gray.
Oh, no! It itches fiercely! It's coming off today.

Birthday cake? It looks more like the Chicago fire!
What ghost haunted King George III? The Spirit of '76.
If Momma ain't happy, ain't nobody happy. If Grandma's unhappy—RUN!!!
I hate being so sexy but someone has to do it.
Sure, I've seen people like you before, but I had to pay admission.
If they don't have chocolate in heaven I don't want to go!
What do you call a person who's happy on Monday? Retired.
God's grace is bigger than my sins.
I want someone to look at me like I look at chocolate cake.
At my age, "getting lucky" means walking into a room and remembering why I
came in there.
Of course women don't work as hard as men. We get it right the first time!
Women are flexible angels. If you break our wings we'll still fly—on broomsticks.
I stopped fighting my inner demons. We're on the same side now.
I lost my mind—and I'm pretty sure the kids took it.
The worst part of retirement is having to drink coffee on your own time.
Some days I amaze myself. Other days I look for my phone while I'm talking on it.
If you don't want a sarcastic answer, don't ask a stupid question.
It's my cat's world. I'm just here to open cans.
Rope. Tree. Politician. Some assembly required.
I found peace of mind the instant I resigned as chairman of the universe.
FOMO = fear of missing out

CHAPTER SIX
ROBIN'S SONGS

Roxy asked me to put some of my best work in here, in their own chapter, so here is a selection of songs I wrote in my younger years. I'm going to omit the worst ones, thank you, but still some will be pretty bad. I'll start with the one I like best, and go at random afterwards.

JACKSON IN SPRINGTIME

You know I'm gonna hit the road.
I love you. Once you loved me.
Another is sharing your load.
Once more my load is for me.

I'll see what I want of the country,
The city, the mountains, the plain;
But I'll be in Jackson in springtime
If you want to see me again.

I know you were happy with me.
Maybe you'll be with him.
But I can't bear to see you without me,
Though I love you all the same.

So if that new guy don't love you,
And you don't know where to go,
Remember I'll always think of you,
Even though I'm out on the road.

And I'll be in Jackson in springtime
If you want to see me once more.
Meet me under the archway;
We'll be together like before.

I'm going a long way, a long time
Away from the one I adore,
But I'll be in Jackson in springtime
If you want to see me once more.
If you want to see me once more.
Jackson in springtime…

[That's Jackson, Wyoming, and its elkhorn arch.]

SAGUARO AND TOMORROW

The tinkle of water in my canteen
Is just imagination, I know.
The lake is a mirage I'm seeing.
Can cactus in such a lake grow?

Who knows when I last tasted water?
Who knows when I last saw a man?
I think I'll give up, and I ought to.
What's death in this hot, burning sand?

I sit in the shade of the cactus.
Funny, you know, it is green—
A symbol of drought and of dust,
Twenty feet tall it would seem.

What does it mean, to surrender,
If not to be less than a man?
The cactus was never so tender;
It lives, and by it I can.

[The saguaro, an endangered species, is used solely for inspiration,
not for food or drink.]

STRANGER IN THE LAND

For many long days
And long, lonely nights
I've traveled to reach this place.
Winter is over,
But the memory is fresh on my mind:
The chilling cold of the mountains,
The absence of game—of all life.
What made me struggle onwards
Save the thoughts of my children and wife?
More snow fell than ever this year.
Trees snapped in the frosty night.
These last days I've seen their shreds
And heard the boulders crack and fall,
And dodged the avalanches.
Now floods and breaking ice show
The signs of nature all at war—
I'd come home, but home was there no more.

CHAPTER SEVEN
LONGER POEMS, PREVIOUSLY PUBLISHED

I promised we'd reprint poems previously published, now that their publishers are out of business. Roxy says she has kept ownership of the copyright on both of these, so it's legal.

THE FEASTER'S DAUGHTERS

Alone I stood, my back turned toward the bank
Where endless waters surge and ceaseless roll;
And it was eventide, and darkling sky
Its pall o'er all the city cast with glow.
Before me stood a tower high and strong,
With gardens round about to show the wealth
Of he or they who builded and who owned.
Just why I stood there I could never say,
For I a stranger to this city was,
And one who knew no one, by none was known.
Perhaps the beauty of the scene struck home:
The tower and the city spread around.
Perhaps the gaiety of feast within
Did spellbound hold me, for I fasted yet.
Perhaps 'twas fate that held me watching still

These two or three of dark'ning evening hours,
For I was curst that I must, ere I die,
Disasters seven helplessly behold
But four of which had already occurred.

And as I watched I knew that here within
Were feasting merrily not few great men
And such as wealth and power called their own.
Their daughters passed me by—did come and go
With serving trays they empty outward bore
But which with meat and drink and sweets galore
They carried back into the tower gray.
I might have been a statue heedless passed
Till one I stopped upon her outward route
To warn about the fears within my heart.
She fought with me and bade me let her go.
I did, of course. The skies were darker now,
And lights within the windows brighter glowed,
And heedless did the maidens come and go.

A pool of murky water close was placed
Beside the tower in the gloomy dusk.
Its noisome waters brown now rose in power—
A column many times my height they formed—
Which struck the tower such a mighty blow
That straightway it, collapsing, fell.

The feasters' daughters wept around my feet
For comfort I could not, but would bestow.
Their fathers, struck in revelry, are naught.
The maidens' grief my heart with pity moves:
Would that the fathers stood out here with me—
Or I were bade to dine with them and die!

SELF-AWARENESS

I

I am.
I perceive my own existence.
What wonders! These,
My hands, my feet, my mouth…
My belly, my loins…
My mind.

II

I perceive
Light.
Let there be sight! Let shine and show.
A world is about me.
A world of land and water,
And an expanse of air above.
Light fills the world.
Light fills my eye,
And shows all things with wonder.
I perceive.
I believe.

III

It moves.
It grows.
It feeds.
It seeds.
It's alive!
(A tree)

Your ridiculous little opinion has been noted.

IV

You!
What are you doing here?
I hate you!
Get out of my world!
Unless you make me happy.
Unless …
We make each other happy?

V

We ought to love each other,
But we're still strangers.
Will I like you if I get to know you?
Will you despise the real me?
Or is, and the poet* says, love [*Orson Scott Card]
Something that cannot help but happen
With understanding?

VI

You make me better than I am—
Wiser, stronger,
Kinder, sweeter,
More caring, more thoughtful,
More considerate, more loving.
Just being with you
Improves me.

VII

Anger
Does not make me kinder
Or more thoughtful or considerate.
I don't like what anger makes me.
It must be wrong.
It must be evil.

VIII

In my quest for wealth and fame
Don't let me forget the difference
Between urgent and important,
Between desire and necessity.
Don't let me forget my priorities.

IX

You came and showed me heaven.
You left and showed me hell.
Now I know the bitterness
Of being alone.

X

Why do I cling
To a world without wonder,
A life without color,
A heart without you?
A great weariness is upon me.
It is time
To return the gift.
I come unto Thee.

ZEN SARCASM:
The journey of a thousand miles begins with a broken fan belt and a leaky tire.
If you can't be replaced you can't be promoted.
Never test the depth of water with both feet.
Give a man a fish and he will eat for a day. Teach a man to fish and he'll sit in a boat
drinking beer all day.

AFTERWORD

Will there be a third collection? Given Roxy's age and the horrid state of her health, probably not. It takes a lot of poems to make a book. She will keep writing as long as she can, though, so anything is possible. Lovers of comic verse can but hope!

Unlike this book whose name is included in the previous, we don't have a third title.

BARBED WISDOM

Be careful of the mark you hit
    When sharpening your nonsense;
If brevity's the soul of wit,
    Discretion is its conscience.

TABLE OF CONTENTS

Claimer:

Poems in this collection are authored by A. Bradbury, and Roxanne Head and Robin Chandler are both pen names he uses. This is his second volume of original verse, the first being *Wisdom and Whimsy* (lulu.com 2007). It is still in print, and can be ordered from the author or purchased at Gypsy Moon Emporium, 1009 East 900 South, Salt Lake City, UT.

Other books by A. Bradbury:

Rell: A Tale of Five Kingdoms (PublishAmerica 2003)

Orphan Rell must marry the arch-magician's daughter. She can't stand him. Can he turn into someone she can fall in love with in time to save five kingdoms from an invasion of dragons?

Faerie King (PA 2004; republished by Create Space)

Fay witch Degolia covets the throne of Oberon, but needs a consort to reign beside her. Her unlikely choice is mortal youth Martin Macadam. Can she turn a naïve youth into a king in seventeen days?

Gremlins 2050 (Bookman 2005, republished by Top Link 2019)

Chance or fate brings young gremlins (corporate espionage agents) together. Their successes bring them internal conflict and outside enemies. Can they unite to take down the biggest crime syndicate in the Salt Lake Metroplex? This is cyberpunk SF at its best, and the book with all the wisdom in it.

Squeezer Jon in the Shadows (Lulu.com 2007)

Orphan Jon Wyenek has been many things in his life: Normal school child, runaway, house boy to a deep netz jacker, and now he's on his own again and looking to support himself as a gremlin. Will he have what it takes to take out the biggest drug lord in the Salt Lake Metroplex?

Red Scorions (Infinity 2010)

Gary earns a cross-country trip in a fantasy land, riding a talking motorcycle. He will be pursued by a biker gang the whole way. I've never read a book like this one! It's fluff, but fun, adventurous fluff. Cover art by Logan artist Newt Ewell.

Emancipator (Xlibris 2008)

Minstrel Shandar errs his way into an empire that condones slavery and sexual abuse of slaves, even children. He decides this cannot be tolerated, and declares war on the empire. What can one slave boy do against the might and inertia of an empire? It depends on the boy... Warning: This is not for those squeamish about subject matter.

Tablets of Immortality (Xlibris 2008)(LitFire 2018)

Myron's friends are turned into vampires, staked and left for the sun. He saves one, and goes to Los Angeles where he helps in a plot to restore an ancient Egyptian artifact that can return the dead to life. Can he and his new friends overcome their challenges and get the tablets to work? This is urban fantasy at its finest.

(Republished by LitFire, with an amazing cover)

Lost Prince Caspan (Four Doors 2010)

The king is dying. The sole heir to the throne disappeared two years ago, and a frantic search is launched to find him. Ragnar, who isn't the prince, devises a scheme to land his butt on the throne that will embarrass and shame all his rivals: a war unlike any ever fought. Can he keep his eye on the prize long enough?

Rescue Mission (CreateSpace 2014)

An ensemble cast is assembled to go to a different world and find spies left there years before. Can they overcome personal differences and outwit the local authorities and the evil aliens who control them? This is Science Fiction at its finest: weird space aliens, flying saucers and interstellar intrigue.

Cortland: A Novel of Jesus Christ

Self-published and available only through the author. Cortland tastes mermaid flesh and becomes non-aging, stuck on his fourteenth birthday. How can he support himself? He finds other immortals, and learns from them. He also finds angel errands and a stone circle that enables him to time travel, and witnesses the atonement of Jesus Christ and the resurrection, as one of the angels at the tomb. This one sells well! Maybe it's the cover art. It is proposed to be the first of a trilogy that ends with the Second Coming. Books two and three are finished but still in editing.

Manuscripts seeking homes:

Zapper

Eddie Vega is inspired to become superhero by his idols, Cyberhero Force. He builds his own rocket pack and ray gun, and goes out crime fighting, but finds he has a lot to learn about gathering evidence and getting convictions. Persistent and brilliant, he challenges a crime lord so powerful that, if he isn't the devil himself, there is none.

Zapper II

Eddie goes to Atlanta to do security at the Goodwill Games, as a cover for his real purpose of trying to locate his parents. An old atomic bomb is set to go off during the ceremonies. Can he and his friends find and disarm it in time? And what will he do when he finds out who set it?

Frog Kisses

Twelve-year-old Cyrus kisses a frog and finds himself in a fantasy world where his name is a curse, and his arch-nemesis the town bully goes with him. Can they mend fences and be friends, so they can save each other's lives on their return?

Frog Kisses II

Cyrus accepts a mission to help the bully's sparewheels grow up as well, and again will fight a dragon at the climax.

Connor's Saga

A minor character in Frog Kisses demanded I write his story, and how he gains emotional maturity.

Sea Wolves

The best of my four successful entries in NaNo WriMo, this follows half-elf Riplakish across country, seeking a place where he won't be plagued by prejudice and rejection. How well can he succeed?

I haven't had any unsuccessful entries in NaNo WriMo.

Cortland Sequel

In the Bible three people call down fire from heaven. Elijah, at Mt. Carmel, against the priests of Baal; Solomon at the dedication of the temple, and the false prophet of the Anti-Christ. That's where this book ends. The first draft is in editing, as is the third.

The Musician and the Vampire

Tarot-reading musician Morgan Gray flees from false charges and finds a vampire sugar momma, Savannah Rivers, and also finds religion. While it contains some of my best, least-forgettable characters, the mix of tarot and faith is hard to reconcile. There is a lot of intrigue and adventure involved in this urban fantasy, set in and around Lost Wages.